Emotional Intelligence

Practical Strategies for Raising Your EQ, Understanding Yourself and Improving Your Skills For Success

Jeffrey Turpen

Your Gift!

We want to show our appreciation that you support our work,
so we have put together a gift for you.
Just visit the link on the last page of this book to download it
now.
We know you will love this gift.
Thanks!

Table of Content

Introduction

"We have two minds, one that thinks, the other feels. These two modes of knowledge, so fundamentally different, interact to build our mental life. "

-Daniel Goleman

An average person during his life is in contact with other people and will soon learn how to relate to them in different ways.

In fact, there are people with whom we can create a deep relationship of friendship/respect, people we hate and people with whom we can only have a professional relationship without any confidence.

These social relationships are often generated by the emotions that these people manage to make us feel. A person can make us smile, get angry, or create a sense of hatred in a single instant. Everyone during his lifetime must learn to manage these emotions to be able to interact with each other in the best way possible and to be able to do any business in the best way.

In short, this person must learn how to handle his emotions. Knowing how to manage emotions is a practice that is often underrated, but that is very important to be able to have a social relationship with many people and to be able to manage an unfortunate situation better.

For example, a man has an appointment with a girl. During this meeting something makes him angry, this person can not act with anger in front of the girl, because he would mean that he is not able to handle his emotions in the best way and this would mean a bad reputation, surely that girl would not want to have A new appointment with him.

Or imagine you have a major university exam. If you can not handle the anxiety and fear you will study incorrectly (perhaps procrastinating in the previous days) and you will talk roughly, anxiety will make you forget all the concepts learned, and the exam will be a disaster because you have not been able to manage emotions.

Or think about when a friend had a death in the family or bad news. You will not try at all costs to speak with him or talk of frivolous arguments because you might irritate him. The ability to perceive other people's emotions is called Empathy and is very important in social relationships because it allows us to adapt our behavior to the social context and to what happens to people around us.

These are just a few examples of how you need to manage our emotions in modern society. Individuals who can handle emotions can develop emotional intelligence, a capacity that, together with the IQ, is capable of delivering excellent results both in work and in the private life of each person.

In this book, you will learn how to develop and train emotional intelligence, manage emotions, and develop empathy.

This path is long and will require sensitivity and spirit of adaptation, but the results will be guaranteed. Every person is born with certain characteristics and a particular ability to handle emotions and understands the feelings of other people, but with a proper study method and desire to improve everyone can achieve excellent results.

A person can be born with more talent than you, but everyone with workout and engagement can produce good results, regardless of the fundamental skills.

Chapter 1: What Is Emotional Intelligence?

"The people with a great emotional intelligence - those who know how to control their feelings, to read and to treat them effectively - have an advantage in all fields of life, both in intimate relationships and in grasping implicit rules that lead to political success. "

-Daniel Goleman

Emotional intelligence is an aspect of intelligence tied to the ability to recognize, use, understand and manage emotionally. To be more specific the emotional intelligence and the set of five core competencies such as:

- **Self-awareness of your emotions**
- **Ability to handle emotions**

- **Self-motivating ability: self-esteem, self-efficacy, and optimism**
- **Perception of others emotional experience: empathy**
- **Efficient management of interpersonal relationships**

Peter Salovey and John D. Mayer define emotional intelligence as that set of skills that include the ability to perceive, evaluate and express emotions accurately and put them at the service of thought and behavior, in an appropriate way to the solutions. The concept includes not only the emotional awareness but also the meta-emotional cognition.

Emotional intelligence prevents anger from turning into a mad rage, or sadness transforms into despair. For D.Goleman, emotions are an integral part of human nature, and through these, we give various answers: with anger, happiness, love. It's the emotions that affect our thoughts and actions, inspire our needs, have effects on our body and affect our social relationships.

Emotional intelligence involves the ability to perceive, evaluate and express an emotion; Capacity to access feelings and create them when facilitating thoughts; Capacity to understand emotion and emotional knowledge; The ability to regulate emotions to promote emotional and intellectual growth. "

A healthy, motivational relationship with a person (a fellow worker, a friend, a companion or a student) motivates us to continue the relationship, to improve ourselves as a person. Instead of a negative relationship with a person immediately becomes a problem.

Emotional intelligence is, therefore, the study of emotions, how to manage them, and how to improve our relationships with others.

Surely some people have the innate ability to understand the needs of other people and their feelings immediately, individuals who can quickly understand the feelings of others and always know the right word but every person can learn to empathize with others and manage emotions.

In the movie "Inside Out" the protagonists are the emotions of young Riley, who can influence her behavior at any time of the day. Joy, Anger, Sadness, Fear, and Disgust can live together when they realize that every emotion is necessary to live life fully.

We should not be afraid of our emotions or try to avoid them because emotions are part of life and build a wealth of experiences that can accompany us for the rest of our lives and teach us precious lessons.

One of the major emotional intelligence experts is Daniel Goleman, who has identified five features.

Self-awareness, which means self-awareness about your emotional state, that is to understand and to know how to express your feelings openly and assertively, to know your weaknesses and strengths, to understand what can be improved and to accept constructive criticism.

But to be self-aware of our abilities also means to have more confidence in ourselves and the possibility of achieving goals,
- Self-control or to manage strong emotions and disturbances to use them for constructive purposes, as well as the integrity that comes from the transparency of genuine openness to others of their feelings, convictions, and actions;
- Empathy, that is, the ability to perceive and recognize the feelings of others, to tune in emotionally with them and adopt their perspective;
- the motivation, that is, the ability to guide and spur ourselves to the attainment of our goals, becoming enthusiastically and positively the creators of our change;
- social skills, therefore managing emotions in relationships and knowing how to read social situations carefully so that interactions, conflicts, and communicative problems are adequately addressed.

All these components allow us to stay in touch with our inner emotional world and consequently to find harmony with ourselves; we also build the essence of the success of interpersonal relationships, the ability to read the reactions

and feelings of others, the skill in solving inevitable conflicts that arise in any human activity.

These features make us understand that emotional intelligence is necessary to have a good social life and for this reason, it is vital to know how to handle these resources in the best way.

Chapter 2: An Emotionally Intelligent Person

"If you can put into words what you feel, it belongs to you."

-Daniel Goleman

Society has often accustomed people to live in a "cage," a path that has already been written and which should provide everyone with a place in society.

Society says that if we study successfully, we will get good grades, these good grades will help us access elite colleges and get the best possible education. We will graduate and thanks to these degrees we will find a great job in a multinational, a responsibility role that will make us make a lot of money, or we will create the next great company.

The summary is an excellent performance at school => you are an intelligent person => you will have a good career => you will be happy.

For this reason, when a student interrupted his studies is classified as a person who does not want to work and never earns money (fake, many famous entrepreneurs never finished college).

Just to name a few:

- **Bill Gates (the creator of Microsoft)**
- **Steve Jobs (founder of Apple)**
- **Michael Dell (the creator of Dell, the largest PC manufacturer in the world)**
- **Mark Zuckerberg (Facebook)**
- **Walt Disney**
- **Coco Chanel**
- **Henry Ford**
- **Jim Carrey**

People who have destroyed this commonplace and have been successful. They were people with great talent, but they also could convey their emotions to the world and intercept the emotions of their audience, giving them what they wanted at that precise time.

People who have high emotional intelligence can understand in a few moments the feelings of other people. A person with emotional intelligence can seize every small signal in nonverbal communication and can quickly become a leader, a mediator and a great motivator because he knows how to communicate with people, highlight their strengths and make them feel important.

Think of John Kennedy when he said, "Do not believe what America can do for you, think about what you can do for America." He makes history with that speech, every single American felt necessary after that speech and showed to the world what emotional intelligence could do.

Here are some good indicators of healthy emotional intelligence. If you recognize yourself in all or many of these points, you probably are into the category of emotionally intelligent people. It's a matter of pride; it means you are empathetic, able to build a genuine contact with others, and you have resources not only for yourself but also for the people you love.

1. People often say, "You understand me."

When a person tells you "You understand me," he is telling you that his emotions are clear to you. You know what he is saying to you, and it is not difficult for you to give him useful feedback.

Somehow, it's like you're reflecting on how he feels or felt in the past, maybe by being able to translate his feelings adequately into words.

2. You can talk about your mental life

Emotionally intelligent people can speak about what they think or feel without thinking about their meaning. In other words, they are not afraid of emotions and have good self-awareness, so it is natural for them to express their feelings.

A component of emotional intelligence is the ability to express your feelings without fear of the consequences. This element obviously does not mean that you have to hurt other people, but that you have the ability to communicate the effect of certain things and behaviors.

3. You can share your emotions

An emotionally intelligent person feels critical to understanding his feelings and considers his emotional life as something to cultivate and investment.

Those who have a closed attitude toward their feelings, instead, show the opposite tendency. This person does not recognize the value of asking for help from a psychologist or a self-help book because he does not consider his emotions as a resource. Who is emotionally intelligent tends to feel things deeper and is happy to talk and sharing it with a psychologist. Exploring their feelings provides these people with greater self-awareness.

A personal growth path (like this book) can help you especially if you want to learn and you already have a developed emotional intelligence.

4. You are intuitive

Emotionally intelligent people understand when at some point something does not work in a relationship.

For example, your partner is angry with you but has not yet verbalized it. In this case, an emotionally intelligent person

will tend to ask, "Are you mad for something?" This proves that he is not afraid to talk about emotions.

To intuit the feelings of other people will allow you always to say the right thing at all times and knowing how to move in any social context correctly.

5. You know when a relationship is over

Notice when there is a serious change in the relationship. Maybe it's the feeling that your partner is cheating on you, or that the relationship is not going anywhere. In this case, like it or not, you know you'll confront this thing and make a decision on what to do.

This skill is precious because it will allow you to don't continue to live in a fantasy world and to face reality. This will end a "toxic" relationship, and you can continue with your life in the best way. You must not interpret the end of a relationship as a personal failure but as an opportunity to be free again and to meet a better person that will help your personal growth.

Do not be afraid to "fail" in your own life, because the real failure is not to admit the existence of a problem and to know when to end a relationship.

6. Do a profession in which emotions are important

Sometimes an emotionally intelligent person chooses to become a psychologist or to perform a job in which the understanding of the feelings of the other is fundamental (e.g., the educator, or the nurse or the motivator).

It is crucial that a psychologist/motivator (for example) is emotionally intelligent because this feature will lead him to provide greater help and greater chances of understanding the emotions of his client.

Even a writer is a person with a high emotional intelligence because he can play with people's feelings to build stories that can excite any reader by choosing the right words in every context.

7. Do you understand why people behave in a certain way

An individual who is emotionally intelligent is aware of his mental life, and the probable emotions that have pushed the other to have a particular behavior. Even in cases of aggressive or self-destructive behaviors, good emotional intelligence allows understanding the motivations that have led to behave in that way. Likewise, if you ask an emotionally intelligent person because he behaved in that way, he will be able to give you a satisfactory answer regarding personal motivations and emotions, just because he is sufficiently aware of his own mental life.

8. You have no emotional preconceptions

If you are an emotionally intelligent person, you tend to ask your friend or partner about his health and emotions rather than feel they already know. You also tend to confront with him about how things are going.

9. Think (and wait) before talking

When the tension rises and the emotions become more intense, people can say things they do not believe. Who has a good emotional intelligence knows that at this time you should think before you say something only driven by anger.

10. You do not feel the need to talk at all costs

Those who are emotionally intelligent know that sometimes silence is golden. He does not feel the need to fill the void with useless words. On the contrary, he knows that it is often better to relax and process things before talking.

As you see these characteristics are beneficial in your relationship with others and it is essential to be able to develop a good emotional intelligence.

Chapter 3: EQ

"Emotions, short breath, and heart that beat to a thousand are the real meaning of existence"

-Franco Califano (singer)

For years, society felt that a person's intelligence was only due to his intellectual quotient (QI), but the introduction of emotional intelligence has changed this conviction.

These studies have allowed us to introduce a new type of quotient, emotional quotient, on which depends the success of your relationships and your whole social life. An important discovery, which was strengthened after a series of studies that have shown that IQ can contribute to the success and happiness of a person for only 20%.

This is why knowing how to develop a proper EQ (Emotional Quotient) is very important to be able to make the best use all the possibilities of success in our modern society.

To develop the Eq, you need to learn to manage your emotions and to understand the signals of your body. Here's how to do it.

Warning: As with any process of personal improvement, it is necessary humility, desire to learn and sincerity. Humility is needed to recognize our limits and to seek help, the desire to learn allows us to learn many new things in an easy and fast way while sincerity will enable us to analyze our emotions without any prejudice, because to understand our feelings is necessary to analyze them and figure out what makes us angry and what makes us happy.

No damage and no fear of being judged, but this book are not for the liars and people who think they are perfect. No one is perfect, and everyone hates liars. If you are not sincere, please do not waste any more time in reading these words.

Without sincerity, no path of personal growth is efficient.

Six skills to develop EQ:

1)   Listen to your body language

Every event that happens around us is handled by the body differently, through physiological changes such as increased heart rate, respiration, or in some particular sensations in some parts of the body.

For example, when you fall in love you feel the "butterflies in the stomach," when you are afraid you may experience a nod in the throat when you are angry it may happen to have very hot ears and flush the blood in your chest.

Getting in touch with your body through observation is the first important step to recognize the effects of various emotions and to put into practice following skills. Body language is also important to discover people who lie. An individual who lies, for example, try never to try to avoid physical contact.

Think of Tim Roth and the TV series "Lie To Me."

Knowing body language is the first step to better understanding our emotions because understanding how they are expressed is the best way to study them.

2) Learn how to handle negative emotions

The ability to manage negative emotions is another useful skill to develop emotional intelligence and live a happy life. When you are under pressure, or someone or something evokes in you a strong emotional reaction, the most important thing to do is manage this flow of emotions in the best way.

If you feel disturbed or angry with someone, before saying anything, you may, for example, take a deep breath and count slowly up to 10. In many circumstances, once you reach 10, you might think about a better way to communicate the problem, so that you can reduce it rather than amplify it.

You never have to talk or act under the influence of anger, because you might say things that you do not think and ruin your relationship with other people. Unfortunately, when we are angry, we want to hurt other people, boosting their flaws or turning to them with an aggressive tone in an evil and unjustified way, just to satisfy our ego.

A person who can not handle anger will not be respected (even in a work environment), an authoritative person who manages to be a leader never has anger, because he knows how to control his emotions.

3) Identify your "hot buttons."

Identify the stimuli that trigger you emotionally and become aware of how and when people touch your sensitive points. Once you determine the stimuli that trigger you emotional reaction use this information to change events.

For example, I jumped like a spring whenever my point of view was not shared or criticized. In particular, my nervousness increased exponentially, if anyone who made such observations was a person I respected and on which I wanted to make a good impression.

Once aware of what triggers you, there are several ways to intervene. One of the most useful is to change the mental framework through which you look at the situation to assign to it a meaning that stimulates in you the most appropriate reaction.

In my case, I learned to look at problems from the point of view of other people so that they can understand their point of view.

For example, when a person criticizes you (a colleague, a friend, or a parent), this person often finds wrong behavior that you can not recognize for ego, mental closure, or because you are convinced that you are right. The opinion of an external person is always able to show us things from a different perspective.

But we must have the humility of knowing how to accept criticisms so that nothing will trigger us.

4) Observe social signals.

People with high EQ(emotional quotient) are more precise in their ability to perceive and interpret facial expressions, the aspects of para verbal and non-verbal communication of other people to deduce their emotional state. Also, they know how to communicate effectively to illustrate their intentions.

Then start listening well to the words and observe the para verbal and nonverbal language of your interlocutor more carefully. Remember that if some emotional states are easy to recognize, others may be thinner and require greater observation capacity.

In literature, a good example of this is Sherlock Holmes, who could understand all of his client's details by just observing them, or Tim Roth in "Lie To Me" (yes, I love that show).

5) Think like other people

Being able to fall into the "world model" to other people is another essential ability to develop a high emotional intelligence. Train yourself to see things from their point of view by considering their values and beliefs (about themselves, about others, and about the world). People will perceive themselves in front of someone who values them by trying to understand them; they will feel appreciated and this will create greater harmony and confidence in your relationship. This ability also plays a critical role in some professions such as that of sellers who must be able to understand the desires and fears of the client and the teachers who must try to understand and motivate their students. Both of these professions are characterized by frequent contact with many people with different characteristics and ways of thinking, and therefore their emotional intelligence is regularly trained.

6) Become aware of your evil thoughts.

To change the way you feel in a situation, the neuro psychiatrist Daniel Amen has developed a simple and practical exercise called "ANT -Automatic Negative Thoughts Therapy" (Automatic Negative Thoughts).

This approach can help you become more aware of the nature of your thoughts and their repercussions on your emotional state. In fact, Amen says, every time you have thought your brain releases chemicals.

Any negative thought releases chemicals that negatively affect your mood. But the opposite is true, that when you make a happy thought your brain releases chemical agents that make you feel good. Dr. Daniel Amen called this ANT therapy by making an analogy: negative thoughts become like the ants that invade the picnic area of a person. If you do not leave them when there are only one or two, the whole ants will infest your picnic area.To avoid dropping your brain into meal for ants, you can practice optimum thinking, a constructive thinking style that focuses on getting the best in all situations and all areas of your life.

Who uses this way of thinking when faced with a problem raises questions like:

What options do I have?

What is the best solution?

Also, optimal thinkers are projected to achieve the best results; they are very productive, have a smart approach to achieve their goals, they can get the best out of the other.

Start checking your thoughts, maybe write a diary, note how many times during your day your mind is bursting with the same unproductive thoughts and apply more and more the optimum thinking by avoiding thinking of negative or unproductive arguments.These are the best ways to increase your QE. In this way, you will discover how to know your body, emotions, and other people's feelings. You will immediately notice the benefits.

Chapter 4: How to develop the five skills of Emotional Intelligence

"When a dawn or sunset does not give us any more emotions, it means that the soul is sick"

- R.Gervaso (writer)

Daniel Goleman, the author of the international bestseller "Emotional Intelligence," suggested that the IE consists of five skills that need to be trained to improve our emotional intelligence.

These five skills are awareness, self-control, motivation, empathy, and social skills.

1) Awareness

According to Daniel Goleman, awareness is the primary element of emotional intelligence. Awareness of emotions allows you to be aware of what triggers emotional reactions within you and allows you to react accordingly.

Conscious people know how to identify the reaction between what they experience and how they behave (example: a friend betrayed me, I feel angry, I beat my friend, I realize that my anger was the cause of physical violence).

According to Daniel Goleman, conscious people have a sense of humor, they are very confident in their abilities and are aware of how they appear to other people?

How to increase your awareness?

Think about the emotions you've experienced over the course of the day and analyze them by writing them in the faithful sheet of paper. Then answer honestly (sincerity, a must for personal growth) these questions:

How many emotions did you feel? What was the most dominant?

The intensity of emotions in scale 1/10?

How long has every emotion lasted?

Have you identified them quickly?

What triggered these emotions?

As time goes on, you will be more and more responsive to these questions, because you will become more aware of your emotions and how they work, enabling you always to be able to understand what is happening in your heart.

2) Self control

Self-control is an essential activity to be able to manage our emotional intelligence.

In summary, it is the ability to manage your emotions and reaction in the best possible way.

People with a strong self-control can adapt in the best way to change, are very flexible and know how to deal with situations in the best way without having any unexpected outbursts of anger or being frustrated. These people know how to relate to others, they are never aggressive or rude and do not make stupid or emotional decisions.

Self-control is fundamental to society, and it is possible to carry out exercises to enhance it, the main ones include:

Regular physical activity to relieve stress

Breathing techniques to improve self-control

Sleep better

Do not overdo the sugar

In the future, we will deepen these techniques (in a new book) to learn to manage anger better and boost self-control.

3) Motivation

Motivation is a key factor in emotional intelligence.

People who have developed their emotional intelligence are in fact characterized by high motivation, know exactly what they want and what they need to do to achieve that result. Their motivation is so high that they succeed in influencing others positively, becoming the motivators and leaders of the working group.

To increase motivation, there are many techniques; the main is to have a goal, plan how to get there, consider a strategy and reward yourself each time you reach a result or when you reach that particular goal.

Just as in Procrastination, even in emotional intelligence, motivation can make the difference between people who want to achieve something and those who are just losing their time.

4) Empathy

Empathy is the ability of people to read the feelings of others in very few instances and to succeed in behaving accordingly.

An empathic person will be able to immediately understand whether a person wants to joke or whether he wants to be left alone. An empathic person always knows what to say and the attitude to be taken in every social situation.

There are two types of empathy, emotional empathy (recognizing and understanding nonverbal messages of others), and cognitive (ability to understand the other person's point of view). Being empathetic means capturing all the social dynamics and knowing how to use them for your benefit.

The best exercise to develop empathy is to talk less and observe a lot more people and their nonverbal language. In this way, you will learn to observe body language and this exercise will help you understand the attitudes of other people by increasing your empathy.

5) Social skills

Social skills represent the set of behaviors to be adopted to be able to relate to other people in the best possible way. A person with emotional intelligence always succeeds in pulling out the best from other people, succeeds in getting them involved and having a trusted relationship with them.

Individuals with excellent social skills can engage people in conversations, with personal questions and listen to the point of view of their interlocutor, they can handle panic and are an example of behavior.

Developing social skills takes time and a lot of training, you will learn to listen to other people and to put them in the spotlight, give them all your attention and your focus and they will put their focus on you. Knowing the nonverbal communication is a great help.

Conclusion

"Emotions: the most important engine of our behavior"

-Bruce Lee

This is emotional intelligence, indispensable in this era of active social interaction. The emotions are significant for every person, and learning to know them is a great help to improve our lives and relationships with others.

We have to think about other people as an opportunity to improve ourselves, not like enemies to overcome to succeed. Only in this way will we develop the best emotional intelligence and we will be able to have a healthy life and productive social relationships.

Your Gift!

We want to show our appreciation that you support our work, so we have put together a gift for you.

bit.ly/2u7pdNL

Just visit the link above to download it now.

We know you will love this gift.

Thanks!